HAMMURABI

BABYLONIAN RULER

Christine Mayfield, M.S. and
Kristine M. Quinn, M.S.

Publishing Credits

Content Consultant/Contributing Author
Blane Conklin, Ph.D.

Associate Editor
Christina Hill, M.A.

Assistant Editor
Torrey Maloof

Editorial Assistants
Deborah Buchanan
Kathryn R. Kiley
Judy Tan

Editorial Director
Emily R. Smith, M.A.Ed.

Editor-in-Chief
Sharon Coan, M.S.Ed.

Editorial Manager
Gisela Lee, M.A.

Creative Director
Lee Aucoin

Cover Designer
Lesley Palmer

Designers
Deb Brown
Zac Calbert
Amy Couch
Robin Erickson
Neri Garcia

Publisher
Rachelle Cracchiolo, M.S.Ed.

Teacher Created Materials
5301 Oceanus Drive
Huntington Beach, CA 92649-1030
http://www.tcmpub.com
ISBN 978-0-7439-0441-4

Printed in Malaysia
Thumbprints.24449

Table of Contents

Destined to Be Great

About 4,000 years ago, a part of the world was in trouble. This area was ancient Mesopotamia (mehs-uh-puh-TAY-mee-uh). The people needed a leader who could bring peace to the land. King Hammurabi (ham-uh-RAW-bee) was the man who was able to do this job.

King Hammurabi did a lot to improve life. He built an empire that brought pride to his people. He made laws that gave peace and justice to his empire. He also allowed changes in art, language, and religion. If it were not for Hammurabi, many of these things might not have happened.

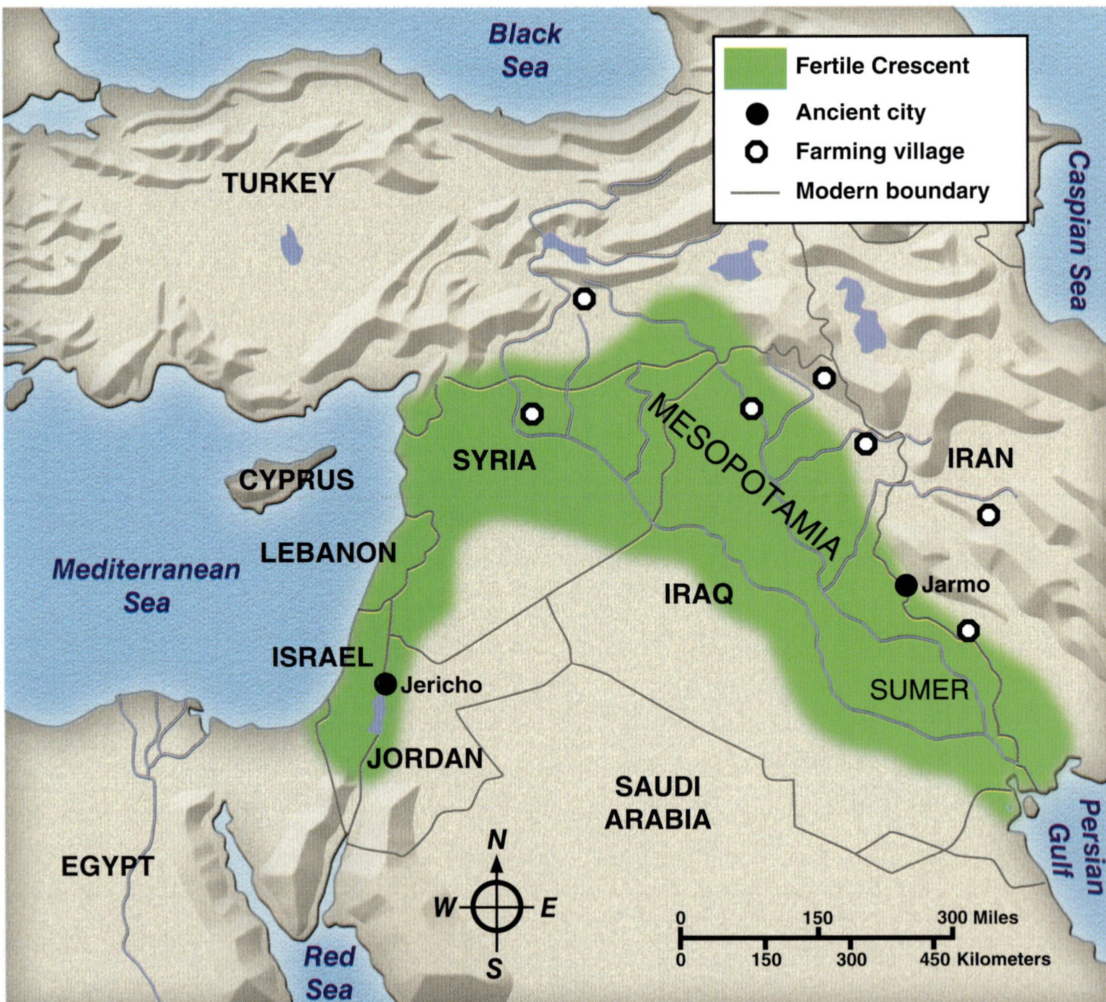

▲ King Hammurabi was a successful leader.

Where in the World Is Mesopotamia?

Today, Mesopotamia includes modern Iraq and parts of Syria (SEAR-ee-uh) and Turkey.

Invading Iraq in 2003

Iraq deals with a lot of conflict today. From 1979 until 2003, Saddam Hussein (sahd-AHM hou-SANE) was the leader of Iraq. He was a very harsh man. In 2003, his government was overthrown by the United States military. Now, the people of Iraq are forming a government. They are working towards being a peaceful country.

Saddam ▶ Hussein

WHO WAS HAMMURABI?

Hammurabi grew up in ancient Mesopotamia. He lived in a city called Babylon (BAB-uh-lawn). After his father died, Hammurabi became king. Hammurabi was a great ruler. He ruled from 1792 to 1750 B.C.

It is amazing that we know so much about him because he lived 4,000 years ago. Many things we know about Hammurabi come from his own writings. Back then, kings were not shy about saying how great they were. They began by telling all the great things they did and why they deserved praise. Hammurabi was no different. He told how he brought peace to the world. He also proclaimed that he was the favorite king of the gods.

▼ Ruins of Babylon

▼ Rubbing made from a Babylonian document

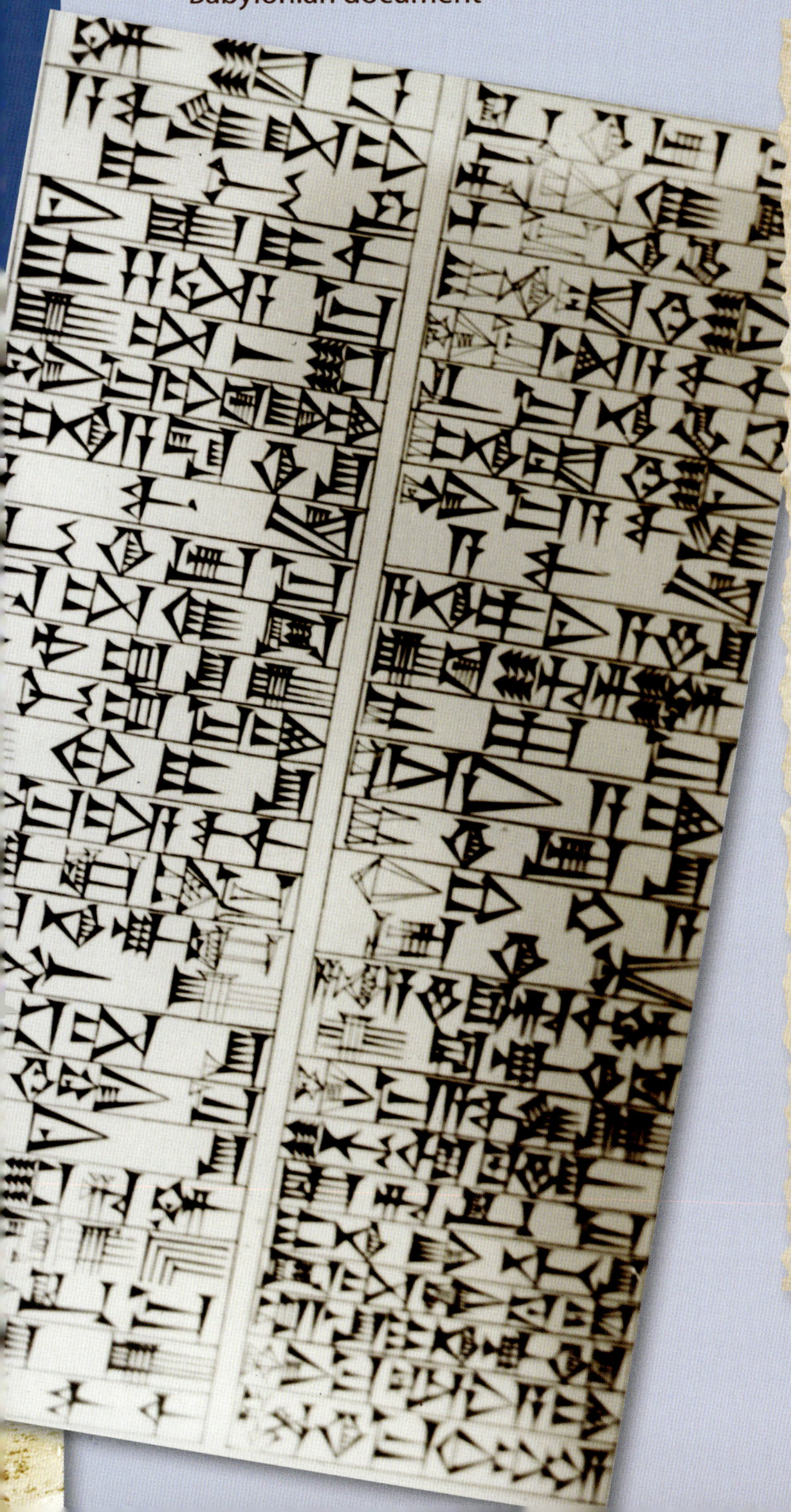

The Bible . . . An Ancient Document

We know only a little bit about the world 4,000 years ago. Some of what we know comes from the stories in the Bible. Many of these stories take place in ancient Mesopotamia. However, most of what we know comes from thousands of ancient documents found there.

Hammurabi's Letters

Hammurabi wrote letters to other kings. In these letters, he described the treaties they made and what he intended to do.

Hammurabi's Jobs

Hammurabi wanted to control more land. He wanted to rule all the **city-states** of Mesopotamia. It only took him five years to conquer the whole area. In no time, the people were living together with just one king. The area that he ruled was called Babylonia (bab-uh-LOW-nyuh). The capital city was Babylon.

As the king of Babylonia, Hammurabi had many jobs. He had to make sure his people had fresh water. Babylonia was near two great rivers. These rivers were the Tigris (TIE-gruhs) and the Euphrates (you-FRAY-teez). To make the river water flow to his cities, he had men dig **irrigation canals** (ir-ruh-GAY-shuhn kuh-NALS). Hammurabi made sure that the canals worked well.

▼ This is a Euphrates River irrigation canal today.

King Hammurabi had another job. He was in charge of all the priests. Priests served the gods. They put clothes on the statues of the gods. The priests placed food in front of the statues so the gods could eat. These were very important tasks. He made sure they were done right.

▼ The Tigris River has always been important in the Middle East.

War, Then Peace

Hammurabi spent his first five years as king winning wars. He united Mesopotamia. Then, he brought justice and order to the empire.

Thirsty?

It is very important to have a clean water supply. Even today, people all over the world get sick when their water supply is dirty. It is a government's job to make sure the water stays clean. That's just what Hammurabi did almost 4,000 years ago.

Improving the Culture

Hammurabi did a lot for Mesopotamian **culture**. New kinds of art developed. Artists started to make pictures that looked more like daily life. Pictures showed birds flying, men fighting, and lions playing.

Scribes copied down all the good stories they knew. One of their favorites was the story of **Gilgamesh** (GILL-guh-mesh). This story was about a king who wanted to live forever.

The scribes all learned the same rules for writing the language. These rules made the language easier for everyone to understand.

There were also changes in religion. The gods people worshipped became more personal to them. They set up shrines in their homes with little statues. They prayed to their gods for protection. Hammurabi built temples for the gods. His favorite gods were Shamash (SHAW-mawsh) and Marduk (MAWR-duke). Shamash was the sun god. Marduk was the god of Babylon.

This tablet tells the story of Marduk fighting another god.

▲ Tales about Gilgamesh were very popular.

Gilgamesh in the Flood

Many religions have a story about a flood. The Babylonians had one, too. In the story about Gilgamesh, there is a flood that covers Earth.

Art All Around Us

This part of the world still has many museums and art collections. The Museum of Iraq has many copper, limestone, clay, and marble statues. Vases and pots were also very popular during the Babylonian time.

A Scientist and A Mathematician

Hammurabi spent time studying the stars and the sky. He realized there were cycles in the seasons. It was his idea to add months to a calendar. In fact, the Babylonians had the first calendar where years were divided into weeks. They even divided the day into hours, minutes, and seconds.

Hammurabi knew a lot about money, too. He made sure that people were fair about trading and paying each other. He even had a system for recording payments.

The Babylonians also invented the **decimal system**. This number system is still used today.

◀ Babylonian Calendar

	Babylonian	Today
1	Nisannu	March/April
2	Ajaru	April/May
3	Simanu	May/June
4	Du'ûzu	June/July
5	Âbu	July/August
6	Ulûlu	August/ September
7	Tašrîtu	September/ October
8	Arahsamna	October/ November
9	Kislîmu	November/ December
10	Tebêtu	December/ January
11	Šabatu	January/ February
12	Addaru	February/ March

$$a^2 + b^2 = c^2$$

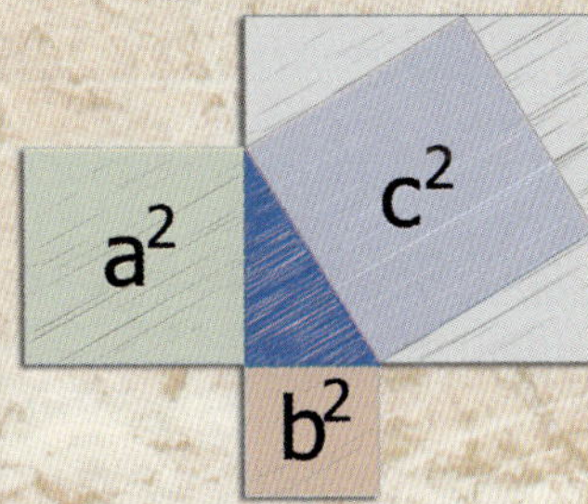

The First Mathematicians

The Babylonians used geometry, algebra, and square roots. The Babylonians even figured out the relationship between the sides of a triangle. This would later become the Pythagorean theorem (puh-thag-uh-REE-uhn THEER-uhm).

Hammurabi's Stars

Do you ever look at the stars? The same stars Hammurabi studied back then can still be seen today! Today, people who study the stars are called **astronomers** (uh-STRAW-nuh-muhrz).

Cracking the Code

After uniting Mesopotamia, Hammurabi decided to make laws. He thought that the people needed one set of rules. Everyone would have to obey these rules. Hammurabi's kingdom needed order so that everyone could live together. So, King Hammurabi wrote a set of laws. Today, these laws are called the Code of Hammurabi. The Code contains almost 4,000 lines. That is about 282 laws. The rules were carved on a stone statue called a **stele** (STEE-lee). At the beginning, Hammurabi says that the gods told him to make the laws.

The Code was written in **cuneiform** (kyou-NEE-uh-form). Cuneiform was wedge-shaped writing. It used symbols for words and syllables. Babylonians did not have paper. Instead, scribes carved on stone or wrote on wet clay tablets.

Citizens knew what the laws were and what would happen if they broke them.

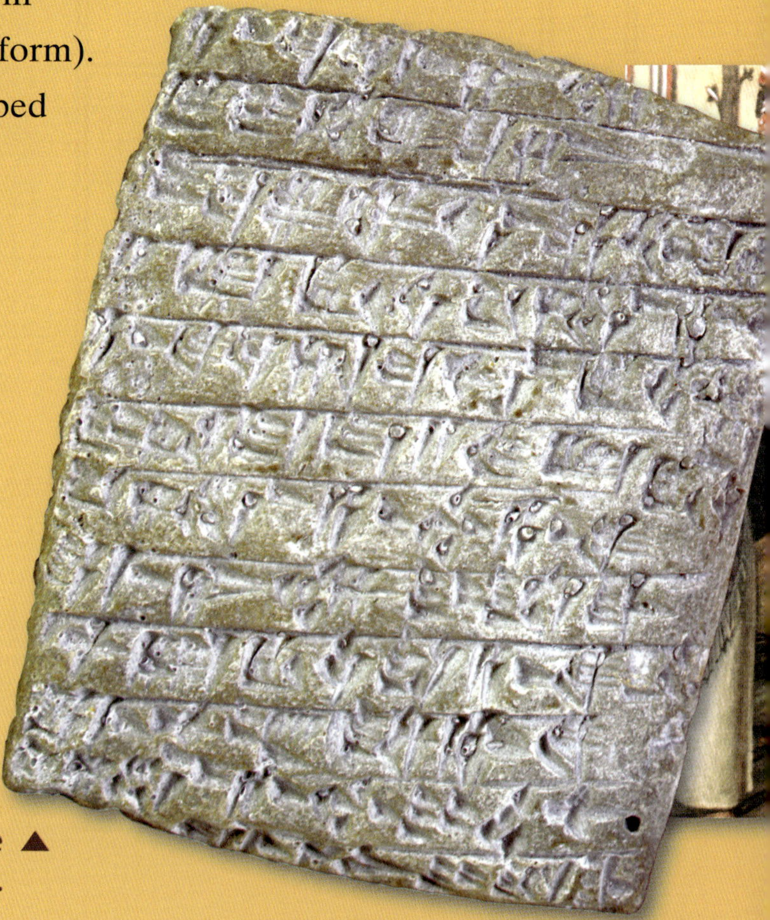

Cuneiform symbols were ▲ etched in wet clay.

The Code of Hammurabi included laws about many different things. The legal process was explained. This way, people knew what a crime was. And, they knew how they would be punished. Even leaders had to be careful about how they used their power. Everyone had to be fair about everything.

Hammurabi Was Not the First

Hammurabi was not the first king to write laws for people. Other kings had written laws, but Hammurabi's was the largest set of laws at the time.

Symbols Instead of Letters

Cuneiform used symbols to stand for words and syllables. We still use symbols to stand for words. Today, symbols are located on signs. They tell us that railroad tracks are approaching, where pedestrians can cross the street, and where to find restrooms.

▲ Hammurabi judges others.

RULES, RULES, RULES

In each section of the Code of Hammurabi, there were different laws. Some of the sections included laws about serving in the army, owning land, or running a business. There were laws for families, barbers, and doctors. There were even laws about growing a garden!

Some of Hammurabi's laws described owning slaves and how to treat them fairly. There was a main message in the laws. The weak should not be hurt by the strong, rich, or powerful.

Hammurabi's contributions are still seen today. They include an organized court system with judges. There were also different departments in Hammurabi's government. Each department had its own leaders. This is also true in many governments today.

◀ Hammurabi set up a court system in Babylon.

▼ The Ten Commandments

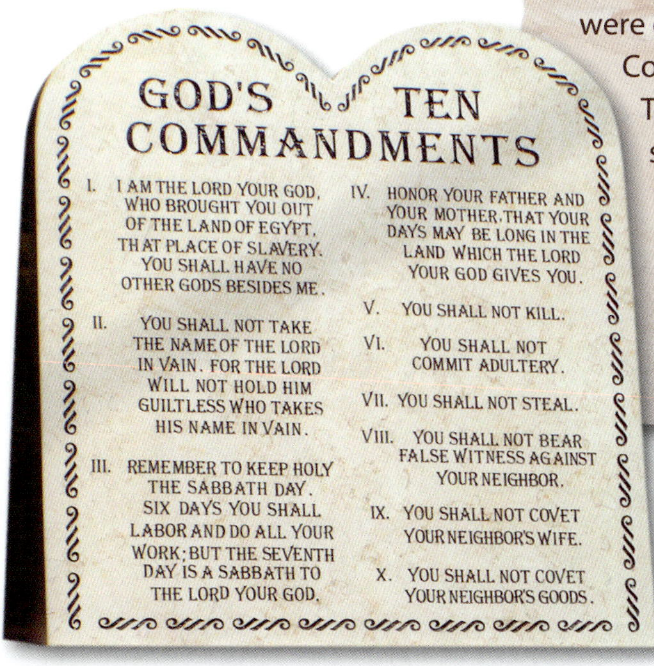

Don't Hit Your Parents!

One law said that if a son hit his father, then the son's hand had to be cut off. No one said that all of Hammurabi's laws were very nice or fair!

The Law of Moses

Moses was a man that may have lived about 500 years after Hammurabi. According to the Bible, Moses received laws that were written on stone by God himself. They were called the Ten Commandments. There are some similarities between these two sets of laws. Both laws were written to make the lives of people better.

We Found It!

Imagine finding a very old and valuable object. Maybe people even knew that it existed. But, they could not find it. That's what happened in 1901. A group of **archaeologists** (awr-kee-AWL-uh-jists) found a black stele. The stele had a picture and writing on it. The man in charge of the dig knew right away what it was. The stele had Hammurabi's Code written on it. People celebrated the new finding all over the world.

This was a very important discovery. The stele helped scientists and historians learn about the time that Hammurabi lived. They learned that the Code was very important to the citizens. It ruled all people. They also learned a lot about the Babylonians and their culture.

If you look carefully, you can see the cuneiform carved on the stele.

Shush, Iran ▲

Shush! We Found the Stele!

The stele was found in Susa, a 6,000-year-old city. The city is now called Shush. It is located in Iran east of the Tigris River. Many Persian people live there today.

Authority to Rule

There is an image on the top of the stele. It shows Hammurabi standing before the sun god, Shamash. This god is the guardian of justice. He is handing Hammurabi his staff and ring. This meant Hammurabi had the authority to rule.

◀ Hammurabi stands before Shamash.

A Ziggurat Fit for a King

Religion was very important in Babylonia. The center of religious life was the **ziggurat** (ZIG-uh-rat). The people believed that the gods visited the ziggurats. Only the king and priests could enter a ziggurat. They were in charge of taking care of the gods that came to visit. Everyone thought this job made kings and priests special.

The Babylonians built ziggurats high into the sky to make it easy for the gods to visit. On the outside of the ziggurats, they built stairs so the kings and priests could walk to the tops. These buildings were huge with many steps all around them.

Ruins of Choga Zanbil ▶

▲ Ziggurats looked like this in ancient times.

Business Around the Temple

The temple was busy each day with people coming and going. The town's business took place in and around the temple.

Still Standing

Choga Zanbil in western Iran is one of the best-preserved ziggurats. During the 1980s, there was a war between Iraq and Iran. Many old monuments were destroyed. But, this ziggurat survived.

Daily Life in Hammurabi's Kingdom

Life was very hard for most people. They worked from sunrise to sunset in the heat. They went home to sleep in houses made of mud bricks. Most people ate bread for every meal. On a special occasion, they might eat dates, olives, or a roasted goat.

When they were not working, the people loved to tell stories. They were also very musical. Some of the instruments they used were the flute, drum, trumpet, and harp. They told stories for entertainment. Then, they added music to the stories. This made the stories more enjoyable.

This Iraqi palace overlooks the ruins of Babylon.

Shamash, the Babylonian sun god

The Gods Are Fighting Again

Many Babylonian myths told of the quarrels that the gods had with each other. These myths were used to explain different parts of Babylonian life.

The World Came from Where?

The Babylonians have a myth of creation. It explains how the Babylonians believed the world was made.

People in Babylon loved music. Drums were used to make stories more interesting.

Other Important Rulers of the Area

Hammurabi lived until around 1750 B.C. His leadership of the area brought great changes. After his death, other leaders worked to keep Babylonia strong.

Nebuchadnezzar II

Babylonian King from 604 to 562 B.C.

One ruler lived about 1,200 years after Hammurabi. His name was Nebuchadnezzar II (neb-yuh-kuh-DNEZ-zuhr). He ruled in Babylon and was famous for conquering Jerusalem (juh-ROO-suh-luhm).

Nebuchadnezzar II was also known as Nebuchadnezzar the Great. He built many great monuments in Babylonia. Nebuchadnezzar is most famous for creating the Hanging Gardens of Babylon. He built these beautiful gardens for his wife. Some of the walls in the garden were 75 feet (23 meters) tall. The gardens are one of the Seven Wonders of the Ancient World.

Nebuchadnezzar II overlooking Babylon

▲ The Hanging Gardens of Babylon

Using Hammurabi's Ideas

Nebuchadnezzar used irrigation to water all the plants in his amazing garden.

The Seven Wonders of the Ancient World

The other six Wonders of the Ancient World are: The Great Pyramid at Giza, The Statue of Zeus at Olympus (uh-LIM-puhs), The Temple of Artemis at Ephesus (AWR-tuh-muhs; EH-fuh-suhs), The Mausoleum at Halicarnassus (mau-suh-LEE-uhm; hal-uh-kawr-NAHS-uhs), The Colossus (kuh-LAWS-uhs) of Rhodes, and The Pharos at Alexandria (FER-aws; ah-lig-ZAN-dree-uh).

▼ The Great Pyramids of Giza, Egypt

Other Important Rulers of the Area

▲ King Cyrus was a strong military leader.

Cyrus the Great

Persian King from 604 to 562 B.C.

The Persian (PURR-zhuhn) Empire reached from Egypt to India. This was a very powerful empire. Cyrus (SY-ruhs) the Great lived after Hammurabi. He conquered Babylon and built the Persian Empire.

Persia was huge. Today, that land is called Egypt, Turkey, Syria, Iraq, Iran, Pakistan (PAH-kih-stan), and Afghanistan (af-GAN-uh-stan).

When Hammurabi took over land, he made all the people follow his rules. When the Persians conquered people, they were **tolerant** (TAWL-uh-ruhnt). They allowed people to keep their customs and beliefs. The people were happy that they could worship how they wanted. That may be one reason Persia was so successful.

Good versus Evil

Persians believed that the world had forces of good and evil. And, people should try to live good lives.

Rebuilding

Cyrus the Great rebuilt temples and buildings. When he conquered a new land, he helped the people there rebuild. He even allowed the Hebrews to return to their land in Jerusalem.

▲ Jerusalem is still an important city.

The ruins of Persepolis (purr-SEP-uh-lis). This was the capital of Persia. ▶

Other Important Rulers of the Area

▲ Rock sculpture of King Darius

DARIUS

PERSIAN KING FROM 522 TO 486 B.C.

Another ruler of the Persian Empire was Darius (duh-RYE-uhs). King Darius wanted all people in his empire to be connected. So, he built hundreds of miles of roads. This made traveling easier. He traveled all over his empire. He thought it was important for people to see their king. Each time he went to a new city, there were parties to honor him.

King Darius organized his land into **provinces**. Then, he set up governors to rule the people there. In this way, he kept his empire under control.

Coins Instead of Trade

At this time, most people traded goods instead of money. Darius created coins so that people could use them to buy things. After this, most people began to use coins as money.

All Should Be Equal

Darius created a common set of weights and measures. This way everyone knew what items should weigh and how things should be measured.

The Persian Empire ruled much of the same area as Hammurabi. From the time of King Hammurabi to the days of King Darius, life in Mesopotamia changed quite a bit. People in the Middle East today still experience the effects of these and other great rulers.

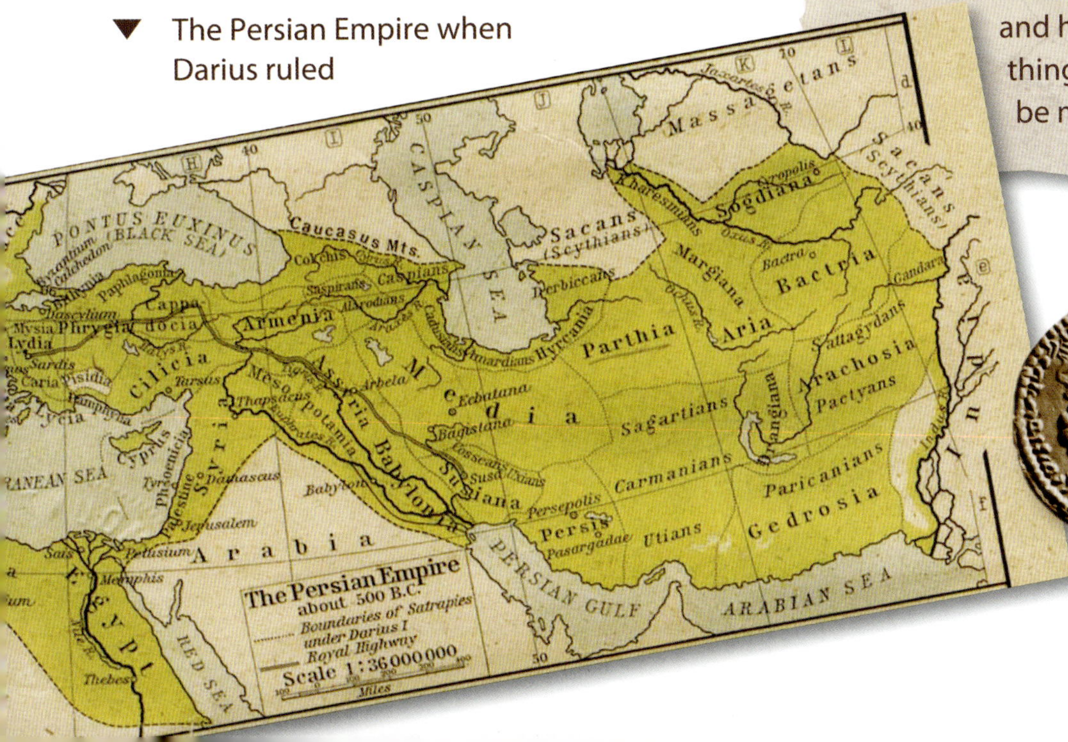

▼ The Persian Empire when Darius ruled

Glossary

archaeologists—people who study historical people and their cultures

astronomers—people who study the stars and space

city-states—ancient cities that ruled themselves independently

cuneiform—wedge-shaped writing on stone or wet clay; used in ancient Sumerian, Akkadian, Assyrian, Babylonian, and Persian writing

culture—people's way of life, including art, religion, music, and language

decimal system—a number system based on the number 10

Gilgamesh—a legendary king; many stories were written about him

irrigation canals—artificial waterways used for watering crops

provinces—territories governed as administrative or political units of a country or empire

scribes—people in the ancient world whose job was to write

stele—an upright stone used as a monument

tolerant—allowing others to act a certain way

ziggurat—pyramid-like temples

Index

Image Credits

cover Time Life Pictures/Mansell/Time Life Pictures/Getty Images; cover Teacher Created Materials; p.1 Time Life Pictures/Mansell/Time Life Pictures/Getty Images; p.4 Teacher Created Materials; p.5 (left) The Granger Collection, New York; p.5 (bottom) Paul Cowan/Shutterstock, Inc.; p.6 The Library of Congress; pp.6–7 Kean Collection/Getty Images; p.7 Ben Goode/Shutterstock, Inc.; p.8 Jiri Rezac/Alamy; pp.8–9 The Library of Congress; p.9 Wade H. Massie/Shutterstock, Inc.; p.10 Visual Arts Library (London)/Alamy; p.11 (top) Mary Evans Picture Library/Alamy; p.11 (bottom) The Bridgeman Library/Getty Images; p.12 The Granger Collection, New York; p.13 Yare Marketing/Shutterstock, Inc.; p.14 B. Speckart/Shutterstock, Inc.; pp.14–15 SuperStock, Inc.; p.15 Miguel Angel Salinas/Shutterstock, Inc.; p.16 (left) The Granger Collection, New York; p.16 (right) ullstein bild/The Granger Collection, New York; p.17 Bonnie Watton/Shutterstock, Inc.; p.18 Visual Arts Library (London)/Alamy; p.19 (top) The Library of Congress; p.19 (bottom) Time Life Pictures/Mansell/Time Life Pictures/Getty Images; pp.20–21 (top) Mary Evans Picture Library/Alamy; pp.20–21 (bottom) Arcaid/Alamy; pp.22 Patrick Baz/AFP/Getty Images; p.23 (top) World Religions Photo Library/Alamy; p.23 (bottom) Graca Victoria/Shutterstock, Inc.; p.24 North Wind Picture Archives/Alamy; p.25 (top) The Granger Collection, New York; p.25 (bottom) Joel P. Shawn/Shutterstock, Inc.; p.26 North Wind Picture Archives/Alamy; p.27 (top) Pavel Bernshtam/Shutterstock, Inc.; p.27 (bottom) Sergio Pitamitz/Alamy; p.28 Popperfoto/Alamy; pp.28–29 The Granger Collection, New York; p.29 The Historical Atlas by William R. Shepherd, 1923; back cover The Library of Congress